Woody's Words

Woodrow Wilson Rawls and *Where the Red Fern Grows*

"I don't care how long it takes me or what I have to do. Some day in my life I will write a book, and it will be a dog story."

LISA ROGERS   ILLUSTRATED BY SUSAN REAGAN

CALKINS CREEK

AN IMPRINT OF ASTRA BOOKS FOR YOUNG READERS

New York

For young Woody Rawls,

school was the farm near Scraper, Oklahoma, where he grew up in the early 1900s. It was the river where he fished, the woods where he hunted, and the fields he helped harvest. All of it was Cherokee land, set aside for Woody's ancestors after they were forced to leave their homelands.

Woody wore homemade clothes and went barefoot. He didn't have much, but he had stories to tell.

"About the only difference between my life and that of any other country boy was that I was always telling stories."

Woody listened as his mama read fables like "The Three Little Pigs" and "Red Riding Hood," but he didn't care much about reading. As he told it, he'd rather roam the hills with his bluetick hound, Rowdy.

One day the mail buggy brought a new book. It was about a dog stolen from his home and forced to haul sleds in the brutal Alaskan winter—a dog who was saved by a kind man and who saved the man's life in return.

When Woody's mama read it aloud, Woody didn't want her to stop.

"When she started reading that night, I was never so fascinated by anything in my life. I didn't know there was anything like that."

The Call of the Wild made Woody a reader. He read it between slopping pigs and picking corn. He read it to Rowdy. He made that hound sit up and pay attention to those words.

That story reached right into Woody's heart and stayed there.

It gave Woody an idea—an outlandish idea for a country boy with no schooling.

He chased after it like a hound dog tracking a raccoon. He wouldn't stop until he made his dream come true.

"I don't care how long it takes me
or what I have to do.
Some day in my life I will write a book,
and it will be a dog story."

Woody taught himself how to write about the things he loved. He didn't have paper or pencils, so he used a stick to scratch his words in the riverbed sand.

With nothing but a hound dog to hear him, he started to tell stories.

"I would try to describe in words . . .
the scream of a red-tailed hawk,
the cawing of a crow,
churring of the squirrels,
the mooing of an old milk cow late in the evening . . .
That was my first writing."

When his family moved to the town of Tahlequah,
Woody went to school some. He won at marbles games and
read as many books in the town library as he could.

Woody's parents struggled to support their seven children,
and Woody helped by delivering milk. His pa taught him
carpentry, and when Woody was in his teens, he hopped freight
trains looking for work. Writing wouldn't fill his belly.

Out on his own, Woody struggled, too.

He had a good heart, but, desperate for food and money, he sometimes stole. More than once, he was caught. More than once, he went to jail.

Even there, he could dream up stories.

Woody wrote when he was hungry. He wrote when he was cold. He wrote in a noisy bunkhouse. He wrote in railcars as he moved from place to place. He pulled paper bags out of trash cans, split them open, smoothed out the wrinkles, and wrote.

"This writing had gotten such a hold on me that I wouldn't let anything stand in my way."

Woody tried writing spy stories and westerns, but he wasn't happy with them. He reached back to his childhood and wrote an adventure story about a boy and his two hounds.

Woody stashed it in a trunk with his four other novels and dozens of short stories.

He locked that trunk good and tight. He didn't want anyone to read his words.

In Idaho, Woody worked in construction, stacked hay on a ranch, and spent weekends fishing and writing.

Best of all, he met a woman named Sophie, who came to the ranch to visit a friend. When they met, it was the right time for both of them. They fell in love and decided to marry.

"That was the day I took off my vagabond shoes and set them in a corner."

But something bothered Woody. His writing might get in the way of his marriage.

Besides, he thought, he'd been foolish to believe he could ever be an author.

It was time to let go of his dream.

Woody gathered up his manuscripts.

He burned every one of them, even the one closest to his heart—the story of a boy and his dogs.

"I was ashamed of the writing. I didn't think anyone would want to publish my stories."

The winter after Woody and Sophie married, it was too cold to work in construction, and Woody grew anxious. Sophie had a good-paying job, but what could he do until spring?

When Sophie asked him what was wrong, Woody decided to trust her with his deepest wish.

Sophie didn't hesitate. She believed in him. She didn't care that Woody's writing was full of mistakes, or that he put an "e" on the end of almost every word. She told him she'd support both of them while Woody spent a year writing.

"I told my wife my terrible secret . . . I told her I had this great and awful desire to write."

Woody again reached back to his childhood. He spent a year rewriting the story about a boy and his dogs.

Sophie corrected Woody's misspellings and polished his sentences. She sent "The Hounds of Youth" to the *Saturday Evening Post*, one of the country's most popular magazines. The editors liked it and published a shortened version in 1961. Soon after, Woody's story became a book: *Where the Red Fern Grows: The Story of Two Dogs and a Boy*.

"He needed somebody to have faith in him." —Sophie

"I thought I'd just forget about it. But you can't. Once it's there, it will be there for the rest of your life. You're a writer."

Woody wanted to make sure that readers learned about his book. In his folksy, plainspoken way, he explained to teachers and librarians how a country boy—without paper, pencils, books, or school—became a writer.

Captivated by his life story, those teachers and librarians eagerly read *Where the Red Fern Grows*. They shared Woody's book with their students. They bought it for their libraries. Woody's words touched reader after reader after reader.

Where the Red Fern Grows became a bestseller.

Woody traveled to about two thousand schools to meet readers. Truth be told, his heart wasn't always in it. Time on the road meant less time for writing.

One day he pushed himself to visit a school in Idaho's Teton Mountains.

As Woody signed books, a small child wriggled through the crowd. He touched Woody's elbow. "I read your *Red Fern* story thirteen times," he whispered. "After today I'm going to read it again."

Woody's story reached into that boy's heart and stayed there.
Maybe he, too, had stories to tell.

"I think I found the answer to it all.
I know now that those forty-something
years of my life ... were worth it."

Wilson Rawls with Stewart Petersen, the boy who played Billy Colman in the 1974 movie, on the set in Oklahoma.

Author's Note

"Woody had a way about him," said Sophie Rawls. "Always had a story to tell."

The story Woody told about a boy who saves his dogs' lives, and how the dogs save his life in return, has found a home in the hearts of millions of readers since its 1961 publication, and still appears on many best book and summer reading lists.

Like Billy Colman, the hero of *Where the Red Fern Grows*, I was stricken by the "dog-wanting disease" as a child. Yet I didn't read his story—or have my own dog—until I was an adult. Just as my daughter was when she read it, I found myself moved to tears.

More than that, I was amazed that Woody, with little schooling or access to books, could write such beautiful words. I'd wanted to be a writer since childhood, and nearly gave up. Woody's dedication to his dream inspired me to write this book.

As a teenager out on his own during the Great Depression, Woody didn't have an easy life. When he was first jailed, at age 20 for stealing chickens, he had 43 cents in his pocket. That he achieved his goal of becoming a published author, even though he spent nearly 20 years of his adult life in and out of jail, makes his persistence even more astonishing.

Woody credited his success to Sophie, who not only

was a budget analyst for the Atomic Energy Commission in Idaho Falls, but his "editor, typist, proof-reader and will-power."

"She made him shine," Sophie's niece, Mary Wedig, told me.

Woody's nephew, Jay Berry Rawls, said that Woody (whom he and his family called Doc) was a true storyteller. "I used to look forward to the time when he was in town to sit on his knee and listen to his stories," he said. "He always had a new one, and it was adventurous, scary, and intriguing for a young person." Woody named his main character in *Summer of the Monkeys* after his nephew.

Woody's niece, Patti Rawls, remembered a kind and attentive uncle who encouraged her to do well in school. She also recalled the off-limits trunk that her uncle would pull from the garage when he visited home and stow away when he left.

Woody's own life story, which he told to thousands of people, blurred the lines between fact and fiction. A true storyteller knows what to leave in, what to leave out, and what to embellish to best serve the story. He'd say he had five sisters when he had four. He'd say his dog was Rowdy, or sometimes Old Blue, though Jay Berry Rawls doubts Woody ever had a dog because of the family's limited means. He'd say almost everything in *Red Fern* was true. And perhaps it was—true to the life he wished he lived. The story he told was the one he wished to tell, and sometimes those are truer to our hearts than the lives we have.

Born on September 24, 1913, Woodrow Wilson Rawls was a Cherokee Nation citizen. As a result of the 1830 Indian Removal Act, Woody's ancestors were among about 14,000 Cherokee people forcibly marched from the Southeast nearly a thousand miles west. During that brutal march, an estimated 4,000 people died. In exchange for being forced from their homelands, Cherokee citizens, including Woody's mother, grandmother, and uncle, were allotted adjoining land in Indian Territory for homesteads. Woody's mother, grandmother, and great-grandmother were educated at the Cherokee Female Seminary in Tahlequah, the Cherokee Nation capital. Woody requested that his manuscripts and other papers be archived in the Cherokee Nation. Tahlequah's public library has been designated a Literary Landmark in Woody's honor.

Woody published two award-winning books set in his beloved Ozark Hills: *Where the Red Fern Grows* and *Summer of the Monkeys*, another story about a boy and his dog. Both have sold millions of copies. *Summer of the Monkeys* received Oklahoma's Sequoyah Award, named in honor of the Cherokee leader who created the written symbolic characters of the Cherokee language. Woody wrote both novels in Idaho Falls, where he and Sophie lived from 1958 to 1976. A statue of Billy Colman and his two hounds stands in front of the Idaho Falls Public Library.

Both novels have been made into movies; two were made of *Red Fern*. Woody narrated the 1974 film and met the actors during filming near his boyhood home.

Woody encouraged children to read and to write their own stories. "Do not get discouraged," he wrote in a letter to aspiring writers. "If you keep trying and don't give up, you will make it someday."

Before his death in Marshfield, Wisconsin, on December 16, 1984, Woody was working on a new story. It was about a dog.

Sophie and Woody with *The Saturday Evening Post*, which in 1961 printed an excerpt from what would become *Where the Red Fern Grows*.

Bibliography

The quotations used in the book can be found in the following sources marked with an asterisk (*).

Anderson, Rob W. "Rawls' Red Fern Memories." *Tahlequah Daily Press* [OK], Apr. 29, 2013, p. 1.

Arizona Department of Corrections. "Historical Prison Register - R." Rehabilitation and Reentry, Aug. 12, 2015.

Bennett, Joan. "Wilson Rawls: From Hills of Oklahoma to Success as Writer." *Eau Claire Leader-Telegram* [WI], Jan. 12, 1980, p. 41. newspapers.com/image/360512939.

Caldwell, Elizabeth. "#1 'How Come Your Book Became a Classic?'" *Flyover Country*, Aug. 27, 2020. creators.spotify.com/pod/show/elizabeth-caldwell4/episodes/1-How-come-your-book-became-a-classic-eio2cq.

*Carson, L. Pierce. "The Birth of an Old-Fashioned Movie." *Napa Valley Register*, Oct. 13, 1973, p. 18. newspapers.com/image/564294122.

Corbett, Bill. "W. Wilson Rawls: Where the Red Fern Grew." *Idaho Magazine*, Jan. 2007, pp. 51–57. issuu.com/idahomagazine/docs/idahomag_january2007.

Curtis, Gene. "Only in Oklahoma: 'Red Fern' Author Once Burned His Work." *Tulsa World* [OK], Oct. 14, 2007, p. A4. tulsaworld.com/archive/only-in-oklahoma-red-fern-author-once-burned-his-work/article_7f6cc7d7-02eb-5add-a5bc-9a5dcd16bc5f.html.

Dayton, Lyman, and Sam Pillsbury, directors. *Where the Red Fern Grows*. Walt Disney Home Entertainment, 2004.

Everett, Dianna. "Rawls, Woodrow Wilson." *Encyclopedia of Oklahoma History and Culture*. okhistory.org/publications/enc/entry?entry=RA020.

For The News. "Colfax Relatives Attend Event to Honor Author." *The Dunn County News* [Menonomie, WI], May 25, 2011, p. A7. newspapers.com/image/542620285.

"Idaho Author Credits Help of Wife in Sudden Success." *Times-News* [Twin Falls, ID], May 25, 1961, p. 8. newspapers.com/image/394511776.

Jonas, Jan. "Leaving His Mark: Siblings Recall 'Doc,' Their Famous Brother, Author Wilson 'Woody' Rawls." *Albuquerque Tribune*, Jan. 4, 1999, p. 15. newspapers.com/image/786359264.

*Just, Rick. "Wilson Rawls." *Speaking of Idaho*, Sept. 6, 2020. rickjust.com/blog/wilson-rawls.

"Keeping Posted: Writer Rawls and His Ring-Tailed Friends." *Saturday Evening Post*, Apr. 1, 1961, p. 92. saturdayeveningpost.com/flipbooks/issues/19610401.

Neff, Bill. "Author's Boyhood Tale Big Hit." *Sapulpa* [OK] *Herald*, May 16, 1974, p. 3. gateway.okhistory.org/ark:/67531/metadc1495275/m1/3/.

*Neurohr, Karen, ed. *Woodrow Wilson Rawls: Writer, Storyteller, Carpenter, Cherokee, Outdoorsman.* Friends of Libraries in Oklahoma, 2011.

Newcomb, Clay. Episode 42: "Where the Red Fern Grows (Part 1): The Peculiar Life of Wilson Rawls." *Meateater*. Feb. 23, 2022. themeateater.com/listen/bear-grease/ep-42-where-the-red-fern-grows-part-1-the-peculiar-life-of-wilson-rawls.

———. Episode 44: "Where the Red Fern Grows (Part 2): Character and Manhood." *Meateater*, Mar. 9, 2022, themeateater.com/listen/bear-grease/ep-44-where-the-red-fern-grows-part-2-character-and-manhood.

Oklahoma State Penitentiary Prisoner Cards: Woodrow Rawls. Oklahoma State Penitentiary Collection 2010.055, Box 19, Folder 4, Oklahoma Historical Society.

Oklahoma State Penitentiary Prisoner Intake Records: Woodrow Rawls. Oklahoma State Penitentiary Collection Ledger 2010.055, Book 31614–32889, and Ledger Book 26610–27873, Oklahoma Historical Society.

OsiyoTV. "Cherokee Almanac: Wilson Rawls." YouTube, Apr. 1, 2018. youtu.be/wEAUd_rx2nY.

———. "Where the Red Fern Grows, A Cherokee Legacy." YouTube, Apr. 1, 2018. youtube.com/watch?v=QbS0L39HmLw.

*Pearson, Howard. "'Ashamed of Writing,' Says Author." *Deseret News* [UT], Feb. 16, 1974, p. 2D.

*Penson, Betty. "Idaho Author Recalls Burning First Stories." *Idaho Daily Statesman*, May 23, 1961, p. 7. newspapers.com/image/724226510.

Petersen, Stewart. Telephone interview with author, May 27, 2022.

Pickett, Connie. "Franklin Pupils Can Say They Know an Author." *Wichita Eagle-Beacon*, Dec. 12, 1981, p. 50. newspapers.com/image/698325627.

Rawls, Jay Berry. Email correspondence to author, June 27, 2022; telephone interview, July 1, 2022.

Rawls, Patti. Email correspondence to author, July 1, 2022.

Rawls, Wilson. "The Hounds of Youth." *Saturday Evening Post*, March 18, 1961, pp. 24–106. saturdayeveningpost.com/flipbooks/issues/19610318/.

———. "The Hounds of Youth." *Saturday Evening Post*, March 25, 1961, pp. 40–56. saturdayeveningpost.com/flipbooks/issues/19610325/.

———. "The Hounds of Youth." *Saturday Evening Post*, April 1, 1961, pp. 34–84. saturdayeveningpost.com/flipbooks/issues/19610401/.

———. "Sequoyah Award Acceptance Speech." *Oklahoma Librarian* 29, no. 3–4 (July/Oct. 1979,): pp. 16–17. cdn.ymaws.com/www.oklibs.org/resource/resmgr/publications/oklahoma_librarian/1979/okl_juloct79.pdf.

*———. "Special Message: For Those Who Want to be Writers." In *Where the Red Fern Grows*. New York: Delacorte Press, 2016.

———. *Summer of the Monkeys*. New York: Bantam Doubleday Dell Books for Young Readers, 1999.

———. *Where the Red Fern Grows*. New York: Delacorte Press, 2016.

"Remember the Removal: Agency." Cherokee Nation, Jan. 24, 2020. rtr.cherokee.org/sites-on-the-trail/agency/.

"Sophie S. Rawls Retires at AEC." *Post-Register* [Idaho Falls, ID], July 2, 1972.

*Tokar, Norman, director. *Where the Red Fern Grows*. Echo Bridge Entertainment; Family Film Entertainment; from Doty-Dayton Productions, 2010.

Trelease, Jim. "Thanks to I. F. Library, Famous Author's Lectures Are Available." *Post Register* [Idaho Falls, ID], 1993, p. A6. infoweb-newsbank-com.welproxy.minlib.net/apps/news/document-view?p=AWNB&docref=news/148F9AAB5C5FB7B8.

*———. "Wilson Rawls: 'Dreams Can Come True,' Part 1." YouTube, Feb. 16, 2018, youtube.com/watch?v=lieGtEFexOc&feature=youtu.be.

*———. "Wilson Rawls: 'Dreams Can Come True,' Part 2." YouTube, Feb. 18, 2018, youtube.com/watch?v=k-zl8OHfly0.

*———. "Wilson Rawls: 'Dreams Can Come True,' Part 3." YouTube, Feb. 18, 2018, youtube.com/watch?v=7JJqnaRVkWg.

*———. "Wilson Rawls: 'Dreams Can Come True,' Part 4." YouTube, Feb. 18, 2018, youtube.com/watch?v=a3QN6CUBdzg.

*———. "Wilson Rawls: 'Dreams Can Come True,' Part 5." YouTube, Feb. 18, 2018, youtube.com/watch?v=DNgcqgRilUo.

"United States Census, 1930," database with images, *FamilySearch*, entry for Woodrow Rawls in household of Minzie O Rawls. familysearch.org/ark:/61903/1:1:XCWX-MMN.

Uthoff, Sarah, S. "Wilson Rawls." *Sarah's Notebook*, Jan. 29, 2021. trundlebedtales.wordpress.com/2014/08/19/wilson-rawls.

*Wedig, Mary. Telephone interview with author, May 25, 2022.

Zubiate, Daniel, director. *Dreams & Memories of Where the Red Fern Grows: A Look Back at the Classic 1974 Film*. Bridgestone Multimedia Group, 2018. amazon.com/gp/video/detail/amzn1.dv.gti.a0b181e9-f143-ffd1-002f-e2e1900a744c?.

Acknowledgments

The author would like to thank Jack D. Baker, Oklahoma Historical Society board member and past board president; president, National Trail of Tears Association; former board member, Cherokee Historical Society; and former member, Tribal Council of the Cherokee Nation; David Cornsilk, Cherokee genealogist; the late Barbara Gutke, teacher, who met Woody when he spoke to her class; Laura Lewis, researcher; Jordan Merica, sensitivity reader, Salt & Sage Books; Karen Neurohr, professor, Oklahoma Oral History Research Program, Oklahoma State University; Michelle Newton, Tahlequah Public Library youth librarian; Stewart Petersen, who starred as Billy Colman in the 1974 movie; Jay Berry Rawls, Woody's nephew; Patti Rawls, Woody's niece; Jim Trelease, author and literacy educator; and Mary Wedig and Jane Zwiefelhofer, Sophie's nieces, for their assistance with this project.

A statue representing Billy Colman, the main character in *Where the Red Fern Grows*, and his beloved dogs, sculpted by Marilyn Hoff Hansen and installed in 1999 at the Idaho Falls Public Library.

For those who have stories to tell and the librarians who celebrate them, especially Karen Baldwin, Roxanne Scott, and the late, great Pat Keogh —*LR*

For Mary Eileen —*SR*

Wilson Rawls with his wife, Sophie, speaking with young students during one of his thousands of school visits.

PICTURE CREDITS

Calkins Creek
An imprint of Astra Books for Young Readers, a division of Astra Publishing House
astrapublishinghouse.com

ISBN: 978-1-6626-8029-8 (hc)
ISBN: 978-1-6626-8030-4 (eBook)
Library of Congress Control Number: 2024947357

First edition

10 9 8 7 6 5 4 3 2 1

Design by Barbara Grzeslo
The text is set in Report School.
The art is created with hand-painted watercolor washes that are scanned and combined with Procreate textures and line, then finalized in Photoshop.